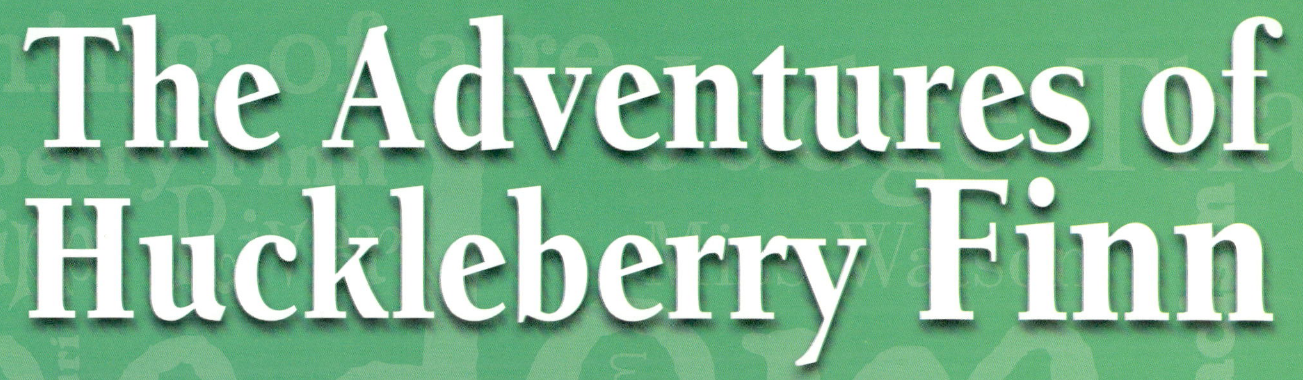

The Adventures of Huckleberry Finn

Lightbox Literature Studies

Blaine Wiseman

LIGHTBOX
openlightbox.com

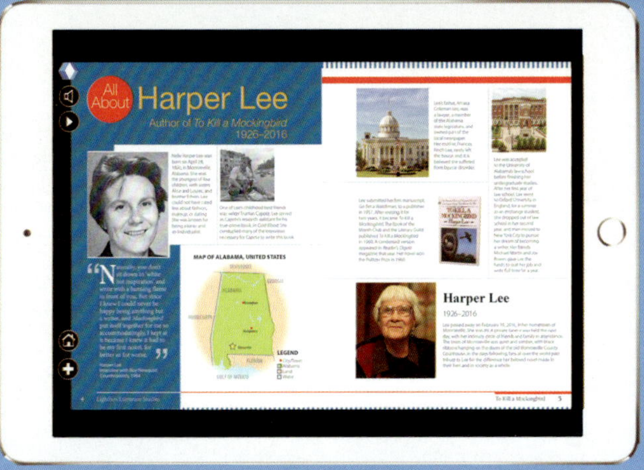

Lightbox is an all-inclusive digital solution for the teaching and learning of curriculum topics in an original, groundbreaking way. Lightbox is based on National Curriculum Standards.

STANDARD FEATURES OF LIGHTBOX

AUDIO High-quality narration using text-to-speech system

VIDEOS Embedded high-definition video clips

ACTIVITIES Printable PDFs that can be emailed and graded

WEBLINKS Curated links to external, child-safe resources

SLIDESHOWS Pictorial overviews of key concepts

TRANSPARENCIES Step-by-step layering of maps, diagrams, charts, and timelines

INTERACTIVE MAPS Interactive maps and aerial satellite imagery

QUIZZES Ten multiple choice questions that are automatically graded and emailed for teacher assessment

KEY WORDS Matching key concepts to their definitions

MORE Extra information and details on the subject

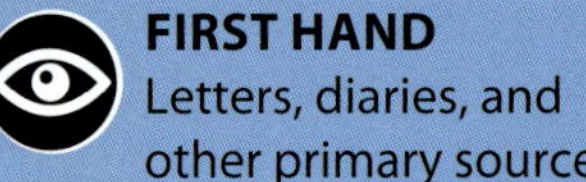

FIRST HAND Letters, diaries, and other primary sources

DOCS Speeches, newspaper articles, and other historical documents

Contents

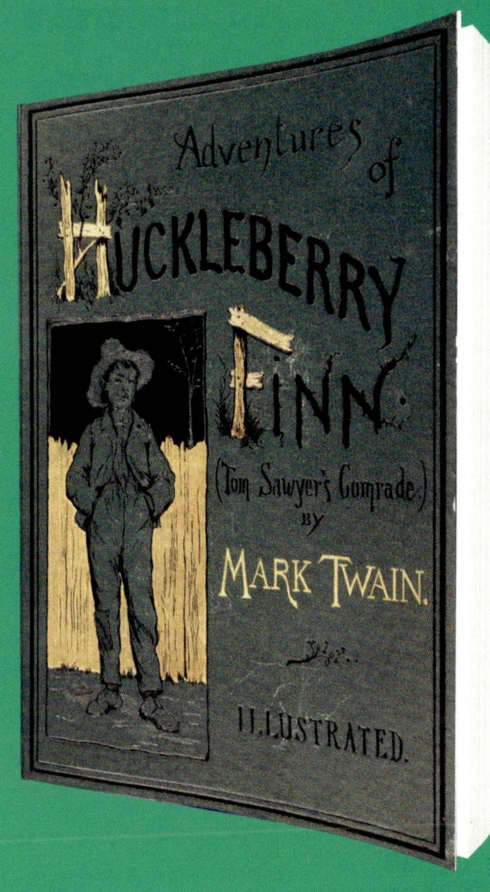
Adventures of
HUCKLEBERRY
FINN.
(Tom Sawyer's Comrade.)
BY
MARK TWAIN.
ILLUSTRATED.

EXTENSION ACTIVITY

Conducting an Interview

Students will conduct an interview with a community member about a time period in their community's history, and submit an audio recording and transcript of the interview. An exemplary interview will meet the following criteria.

- Clearly defines the purpose of the interview
- Conducts thorough background research to inform the focus of the interview and the questions
- Drafts a complete list of thoughtful, in-depth, and varied questions prior to the interview
- Interviews a subject with relevant knowledge on the topic and time period in question
- Asks questions in a logical order, building upon each other
- Treats the interview subject in a polite, respectful, and professional manner
- Does not interrupt or rush the interview subject
- Shows interest and enthusiasm in responses and follow-up questions
- Chooses follow-up questions that demonstrate active listening
- Asks for clarification and further details when necessary
- Asks questions about personal experiences related to the topic
- Asks questions regarding factual information and the interview subject's opinion on the topic
- Asks creative questions that reflect fresh insights on the topic
- Records the full interview in a quiet environment
- Organizes and edits the interview transcript to be clear and factual

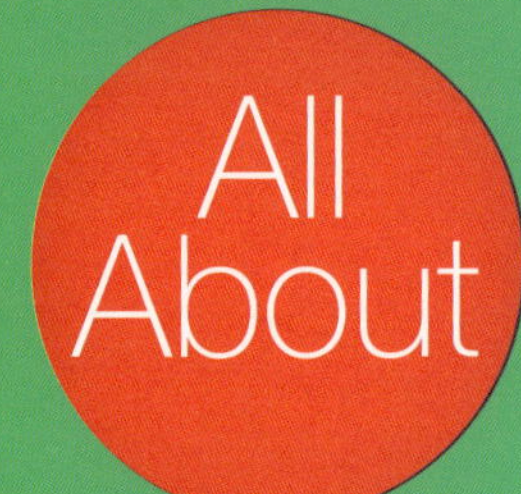

Mark Twain

Author of *The Adventures of Huckleberry Finn*
1835–1910

Mark Twain is one of the most celebrated authors in American history. Known for his smart, humorous observations, Twain's writings featured groundbreaking commentaries on American life in the nineteenth century. Throughout his life, he traveled around the United States and the world. These adventures inspired the stories in his literary classics.

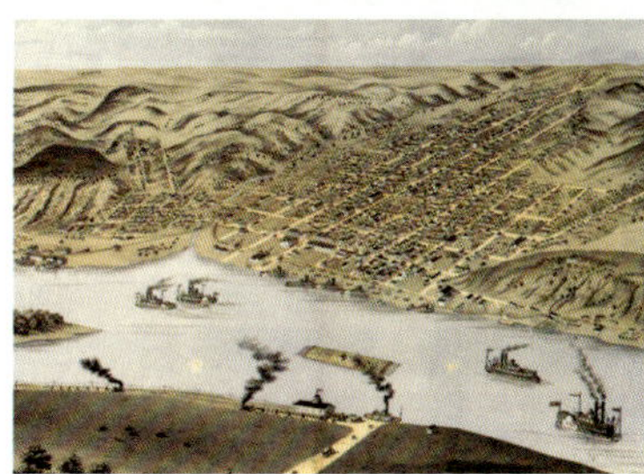

Born in 1835 in the village of Florida, Missouri, Twain's real name was Samuel Langhorne Clemens. When he was four years old, the family moved to the nearby town of Hannibal, Missouri, on the banks of the Mississippi River.

> **"The coat of arms of the human race ought to consist of a man with an axe on his shoulder proceeding toward a grindstone. Or, it ought to represent the several members of the human race holding out the hat to each other. For we are all beggars. Each in his own way."**
>
> Mark Twain,
> *Autobiography of Mark Twain: Volume One*

MAP OF MISSOURI, UNITED STATES

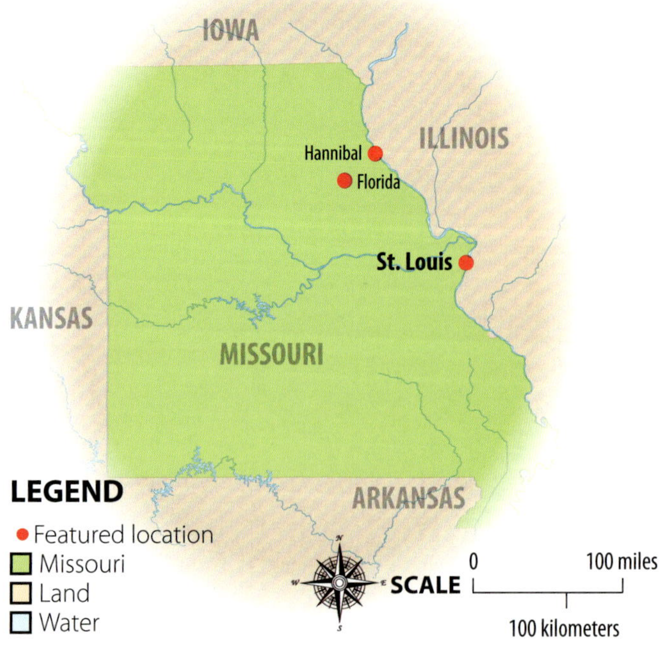

Samuel's father, John Clemens, was a serious man who worked hard at a variety of jobs to provide for the family. It was from his mother, Jane, that Samuel inherited his sense of adventure. In 1847, John Clemens died of pneumonia. Without their **breadwinner**, the family fell into desperate poverty. Samuel was forced to leave school and find work. He joined the *Hannibal Courier* newspaper as a printer's **apprentice**.

WESTERN UNION.

CITY OF HANNIBAL, MO., NOVEMBER 21, 1850.

A few years later, Clemens began writing and editing for his brother's newspaper, the *Hannibal Western Union*. At age 21, he made a career change, taking him on adventures that would inspire his greatest novels. Working as a steamboat pilot on the Mississippi River, Clemens met many interesting characters. It was here that he found his pseudonym. "Mark twain" was a term used by boatmen on the Mississippi. It meant that the water in a particular area was 12 feet (3.7 meters), or two fathoms, deep.

Clemens loved his work on the Mississippi, but he was forced to leave when the American Civil War broke out in 1861. He briefly joined a Confederate troop, but left military life soon after. He and his brother headed west, looking for adventure and riches in the California gold rush. Gold mining did not work out the way he had hoped, and Clemens began writing again.

Working as a journalist in San Francisco, California, Clemens began publishing stories under the name Mark Twain. His short stories and travelogues were printed in newspapers around the country, and led to his first novel, *The Innocents Abroad*, published in 1869. Twain became an instant celebrity. His fans eagerly awaited his next works, and he was able to travel around the United States and the world entertaining enthusiastic crowds.

TEACHER NOTES

Google Maps

Hannibal, Missouri

Use street view to explore Hannibal, Missouri, on the Mississippi River. Today, Twain's hometown features the Mark Twain Riverboat, Becky Thatcher's Diner, and The Mark Twain Boyhood Home & Museum.

First Hand

Have We Misread Huckleberry Finn?: Interview of Andrew Levy

Examine this interview with professor Andrew Levy from *American History Magazine* about Mark Twain and *The Adventures of Huckleberry Finn*.

1. What types of questions does the interviewer ask? What topics does he focus on? Why would he focus on these specific areas?
2. Levy believes that many critics have missed Twain's real message. Do you agree with this assertion? Why or why not? What you do think the novel's message is and why? Cite textual evidence to support your position.
3. Levy claims that the novel is not about progress, but about history coming around. What do you think this means? Is he correct? Why do you think so?

EXTENSION ACTIVITY

Researching for a Writing Assignment

Students will complete a thorough research process to prepare for a writing assignment, and organize their research in a logical manner that supports their writing. An exemplary research process will meet the following criteria.

- Creates a goal for the research, based on the topic and working thesis
- Creates specific, thoughtful, and inventive research questions that are relevant to the topic of the writing assignment
- Produces a list of categories, key words, and related ideas to effectively assist in researching
- Uses high-quality sources that pertain to the topic and come in a variety of formats, such as books, journals, primary sources, websites, and databases
- Determines accuracy of all sources
- Uses sources that provide balanced research and various perspectives on the topic in question
- Takes notes to highlight the key facts and ideas in order to answer all research questions
- Extracts relevant, detailed information from the sources during the note-taking process
- Organizes the research notes in a clear and concise manner
- Organizes the research notes logically and in a way that sets up the information and ideas for analysis and the writing process
- Analyzes the information and produces ideas and points to support the working thesis
- Uses an effective and suitable format to present all research
- Properly cites all sources used

Setting of the Novel

Snapshot

Hannibal, Missouri
Current Population 17,916

In **1830**, only **30 people** lived in the village of Hannibal, Missouri. Twenty years later, it was a city, and home to more than **2,000 people**.

By **1840**, more than **1,000 steamboats** arrived in Hannibal each year, bringing people and products to the bustling town.

In **1857**, Clemens met a well-known steamboat pilot named Horace Bixby. He paid Bixby **$500** to train him as a pilot.

The Adventures of Huckleberry Finn is set on the Mississippi River. The fictional town where the story begins is called St. Petersburg, Missouri. This town is based on Twain's childhood hometown of Hannibal. The mid-nineteenth century was a **tumultuous** time in the United States, especially in the South. Slavery was still commonplace during Twain's childhood, and poverty was another prevalent issue. The slaves, slavers, gamblers, con artists, and fugitives featured in *The Adventures of Huckleberry Finn* were all inspired by real-life people and events Twain encountered in Hannibal and on his travels along the Mississippi.

The Fictional Town of St. Petersburg

"Well, when Tom and me got to the edge of the hill-top, we looked away down into the village and could see three or four lights twinkling, where there was sick folks, may be; and the stars over us was sparkling ever so fine; and down by the village was the river, a whole mile broad, and awful still and grand. We went down the hill and found Jo Harper, and Ben Rogers, and two or three more of the boys, hid in the old tanyard. So we unhitched a skiff and pulled down the river two mile and a half, to the big scar on the hillside, and went ashore."

Huckleberry Finn, Chapter II

The happiest memories of Twain's childhood involved the river. He wrote that his greatest ambition was "to be a steamboatman." Working on a Mississippi River steamboat was a prestigious career full of adventure. Twain and his childhood friends would dream of one day piloting the classic boats down this iconic river.

As a child growing up in Hannibal, Twain was also exposed to the brutality of slavery firsthand. He witnessed the senseless murder of a slave by a white man. Twain also remembered seeing a group of slaves chained together, waiting on the docks to be sold. These experiences left a lasting impression on the author. Remembering the slaves on the docks, Twain wrote, "those were the saddest faces I have ever seen."

TEACHER NOTES

Video

The Adventures of Huckleberry Finn Part 1: Crash Course Literature #302
Find out more about Mark Twain and *The Adventures of Huckleberry Finn* by watching this video.

1. Why is it important to understand that Huck believes turning Jim in is the ethically correct thing to do? Describe the tension between Huck's conscience and the social order. How does he overcome this tension?
2. Why were early reviews of the novel so negative? Despite criticism against it, the book is considered significant by many people, especially today. Why do you think this is the case?

Weblink

Mapping Huckleberry Finn's Mississippi River Journey
Review the article by Andrew DeGraff about Huck's route along the Mississippi River.

1. Why is the setting of the novel so important? How would the story be affected if it were set in a different location? Provide reasons for your answer.
2. How is Huck's journey down the river related to his internal journey? What parallels can you draw between them?
3. What does the river mean to Jim? Explain its significance in your own words.

EXTENSION ACTIVITY

Analyzing a Newspaper Article

Students will assess a newspaper article and write an analysis. An exemplary analysis will meet the following criteria.

- Identifies the topic of the article
- Identifies the main points and opinions presented in the article
- Identifies the writer of the article
- Presents information about the writer and infers how his or her life may have shaped this opinion
- Assesses the writer's reliability
- Analyzes how the writer makes his or her argument
- Uses evidence from the article to show how the writer supports his or her argument
- Analyzes the writer's use of literary devices to enhance the article
- Differentiates between the facts and opinions presented in the article
- Identifies when and where the article was published, and determines its intended audience
- Identifies and understands the goals of the article
- Assesses the effectiveness of the format (a newspaper opinion article) in presenting the writer's argument
- Connects the article to the societal and historical context in which it was written
- Infers what is not said about this topic in the article
- Identifies what information is unintentionally implied in the article
- Infers what other opinions may be presented about this topic and who may be most likely to express them
- Uses a number of other resources to analyze the context of the article

Time Period of the Novel

The Adventures of Huckleberry Finn was published in 1884, 20 years after slavery was **abolished** in the United States. However, Twain had been working on the book for years. He based it around the time of his childhood in the 1830s and 1840s, when slavery was still legal in several states, including Missouri. Slavery began in the United States in 1619, when African slaves were brought to the Jamestown Colony in what is now Virginia. Slave labor was a major part of the U.S. economy. This was especially true in the South, which had an ideal climate for growing cotton.

Freedom

"Jim talked out loud all the time while I was talking to myself. He was saying how the first thing he would do when he got to a free state he would go to saving up money and never spend a single cent, and when he got enough he would buy his wife, which was owned on a farm close to where Miss Watson lived; and then they would both work to buy the two children, and if their master wouldn't sell them, they'd get an Ab'litionist to go and steal them.

It most froze me to hear such talk. He wouldn't ever dared to talk such talk in his life before. Just see what a difference it made in him the minute he judged he was about free."

Huckleberry Finn, Chapter XVI

Southern plantation owners used slaves to grow, pick, and process cotton for use in the **textile** industry. Processing included the slow and painstaking job of removing seeds from the cotton. In 1793, a tool called the cotton gin revolutionized this process. Now, cotton seeds could be removed much more quickly. Cotton soon became the largest and most important industry in the South. Plantations grew bigger, and their owners grew rich, as they brought in more slaves to pick more cotton. By 1840, there were nearly 2.5 million slaves in the country. Almost 60,000 of them lived in Missouri.

Across the river from Missouri was Illinois, a free state. With freedom so close, it was tempting for slaves to run away. It was not easy, however. If runaway slaves were captured, they could be sent back, sold to another slave owner, beaten, or even killed. For many, it was worth the risk. The **Underground Railroad** helped thousands of people escape slavery and gain their freedom, but many others were caught in the process.

While slavery was formally abolished before the novel was published, the issue was far from over. Four million slaves had been **emancipated**, but they were not necessarily free. Many southern states passed laws known as "black codes." These codes were designed to restrict the rights of former slaves. Extremist groups such as the Ku Klux Klan grew out of this environment, and racial tension only grew in the South. Violence, oppression, and racism did not end with the Civil War. The country's history of slavery continues to influence and shape American culture even today.

TEACHER NOTES

Video

How and Why We Read: Crash Course English Literature #1

Discover how and why people read by watching this video.

1. What is the point of reading critically? Explain the importance of this in your own words.
2. Do you agree with John that authorial intent does not matter? Why or why not?

Document

The 100 best novels: No 23 – The Adventures of Huckleberry Finn by Mark Twain (1884/5)

Examine this article from *The Guardian* by Robert McCrum.

1. What stance, if any, does the author take?
2. Why do you think *The Adventures of Huckleberry Finn* was ranked number 23 on the list of the 100 best novels? Do you agree with this ranking? Why or why not?

EXTENSION ACTIVITY

Writing a Short Story

Students will choose an excerpt from the novel and use it as their inspiration in writing a short story. An exemplary short story will meet the following criteria.

- Engages the reader from the opening line
- Establishes a clear, consistent point of view
- Introduces a narrator and a setting
- Develops an engaging conflict at the heart of the narrative to build tension and keep the reader interested
- Develops characters and events through purposeful and well-crafted literary devices
- Creates a logical progression of events in the narrative that build upon each other using various techniques
- Explores ideas, concepts, and writing styles with creativity and originality
- Demonstrates a high level of skill in using appropriate narrative techniques to tell the story
- Concludes the narrative in a thoughtful, effective manner appropriate to the narrative
- Uses varied, purposeful diction and syntax to affect style and serve the narrative
- Writes with clarity, imagination, and a unique, personal voice
- Does not use stereotypes or clichés
- Uses effective, believable dialogue
- Uses correct spelling, grammar, and punctuation

Conflict in the Novel

Great stories are driven by conflict. Many literary classics feature a battle between good and evil. Other stories tell of regular people becoming legends by surviving against all odds. Some of the most beloved characters in literature have struggled with a moral dilemma, while others have sacrificed everything to defeat their oppressors. Conflict in literature leads to lessons learned and resolutions that can change the minds of characters and readers alike.

The Four Major Types of Conflict in Literature

MAN VS. MAN

A major form of conflict used in literature features one character struggling against another. The book *12 Years a Slave* is written by, and about, a free man named Solomon Northup. The protagonist, who is captured and sold into slavery, comes into conflict with several people throughout the book, including a ruthless slave master named Edwin Epps.

MAN VS. SELF

A common way for writers to raise questions of morality is by creating conflict between a character and their own beliefs. In *Uncle Tom's Cabin* by Harriet Beecher Stowe, a slave owner named Augustine St. Clare struggles with the morality of owning slaves.

MAN VS. SOCIETY

Sometimes, a character will struggle to find a place within society. Issues of morality and political disputes are examples of man versus society conflict. In *Someone Knows My Name (The Book of Negroes)* by Lawrence Hill, the main character, Aminata, struggles against society to gain her freedom from slavery.

MAN VS. NATURE

Adventure stories often contain a struggle between a character and natural forces. Weather, animals, geographic features, or natural disasters can challenge characters to move, adapt, or survive. Joseph Conrad's *Heart of Darkness* is a tale filled with conflict. Among other conflicts, the characters also struggle against the elements of colonial Africa.

Types of Conflict in *The Adventures of Huckleberry Finn*

The two main types of conflict in *The Adventures of Huckleberry Finn* are man versus society and man versus self. Both of these conflicts play a major role in the novel.

Man versus Society

"It was kind of lazy and jolly, laying off comfortable all day, smoking and fishing, and no books nor study. Two months or more run along, and my clothes got to be all rags and dirt, and I didn't see how I ever got to like it so well at the widow's, where you had to wash, and eat on a plate, and comb up, and go to bed and get up regular, and be forever bothering over a book and have old Miss Watson pecking at you all the time. I didn't want to go back no more."

Huckleberry Finn, Chapter VI

Man versus Self

"They went off, and I got aboard the raft, feeling bad and low, because I knowed very well I had done wrong, and I see it warn't no use for me to try and do right; a body that don't get started right when he's little ain't got no show—when the pinch comes there ain't nothin' to back him up and keep him to his work and so he gets beat. Then I thought a minute, and says to myself, hold on, —s'pose you'd a done right and give Jim up; would you felt better than you do now? No, says I, I'd feel bad—I'd feel just the same way I do now. Well, then, says I, what's the use you learning to do right when it's troublesome to do right and ain't no trouble to do wrong, and the wages is just the same? I was struck. I couldn't answer that."

Huckleberry Finn, Chapter XVI

TEACHER NOTES

More

The Types of Conflict in *The Adventures of Huckleberry Finn*

Analyze the excerpts from the novel revealing the types of conflict as they appear in *The Adventures of Huckleberry Finn*.

1. How do these excerpts of conflict reveal the novel's theme? How do they reveal character? Explain and defend your ideas.
2. Write an analysis of Twain's development of conflict between Pap and Huck. What deeper truths may be suggested about these characters as a result of their conflict?

Video

Conflict in Literature

Explore the four different kinds of literary conflict in this video.

1. Explain each of the four types of conflicts in your own words. Provide examples of each. They can be from plays, novels, short stories, films, or television shows.
2. What is the difference between an internal conflict and an external conflict? Can you think of any similarities between them?

EXTENSION ACTIVITY

Analyzing Bias in a Document

Students will analyze the bias that exists in a document from a different historical time and place, and how that bias shapes the opinions presented in the document. An exemplary analysis of bias in a document will meet the following criteria.

- Identifies the main points presented in the document
- Offers an in-depth interpretation of the document
- Differentiates between facts and opinions
- Identifies the writer
- Presents information about the writer
- Assesses the writer's reliability
- Determines the goals for the document
- Considers and assesses the writer's perspective
- Determines the writer's intended audience
- Identifies when and where the document was written
- Describes the historical context for the time and place in which the document was created, and analyzes how this context might have shaped the opinions expressed in the document
- Infers political or societal influences that may have shaped the opinions presented in the document
- Determines whether the writer had first-hand knowledge of the topic or event, or whether they are reporting as a secondary source
- Determines the document's bias
- Infers what interests the writer might have had that led them to create this document
- Explores other sources related to the topic of the document

Introducing the Characters

Twain created some of the most memorable and beloved characters in all of American literature. He often based these characters on people he met in real life or adapted them from tales he heard during his travels. Twain was a master at making heroes of underdogs and of ridiculing those in power. Characters such as Huckleberry Finn and Jim are simple, yet wise. Despite their unorthodox ways of life, they always end up making the right decision. These flawed heroes are relatable to most readers. They do more than simply tell the story of a trip down the Mississippi River. They also take readers along for the ride.

Major Characters in *The Adventures of Huckleberry Finn*

Huckleberry Finn
The 14-year-old protagonist of the novel who sets off down the Mississippi River to escape an abusive father and a restrictive society.

Jim
The runaway slave traveling down the river with Huck, seeking his freedom.

The Adventures of Huckleberry Finn is narrated by Huck, the novel's main character, or protagonist. By telling a story through the perspective of its characters, a writer gives the reader the opportunity to share the experiences, understand the viewpoints, and interpret the lessons presented in the narrative. Huck does not outwardly judge the world around him, but merely tells the reader what he sees and feels as the story unfolds. He does judge his own interpretation of the events in the story. He wonders how his actions would be viewed by other characters in the book and then comes to his own conclusions. This sense of resolute self-doubt has made Huck Finn one of literature's most endearing characters for more than 130 years.

The other characters in the novel give readers an idea of the environment Huck lives in and why he views the world in a particular way. In Huck's simplified view of society, the Widow Douglas represents civilization, while Pap Finn represents authority. Huck distrusts these phenomena because he feels misunderstood and mistreated by the people who represent them. Jim and Tom, on the other hand, represent freedom and adventure.

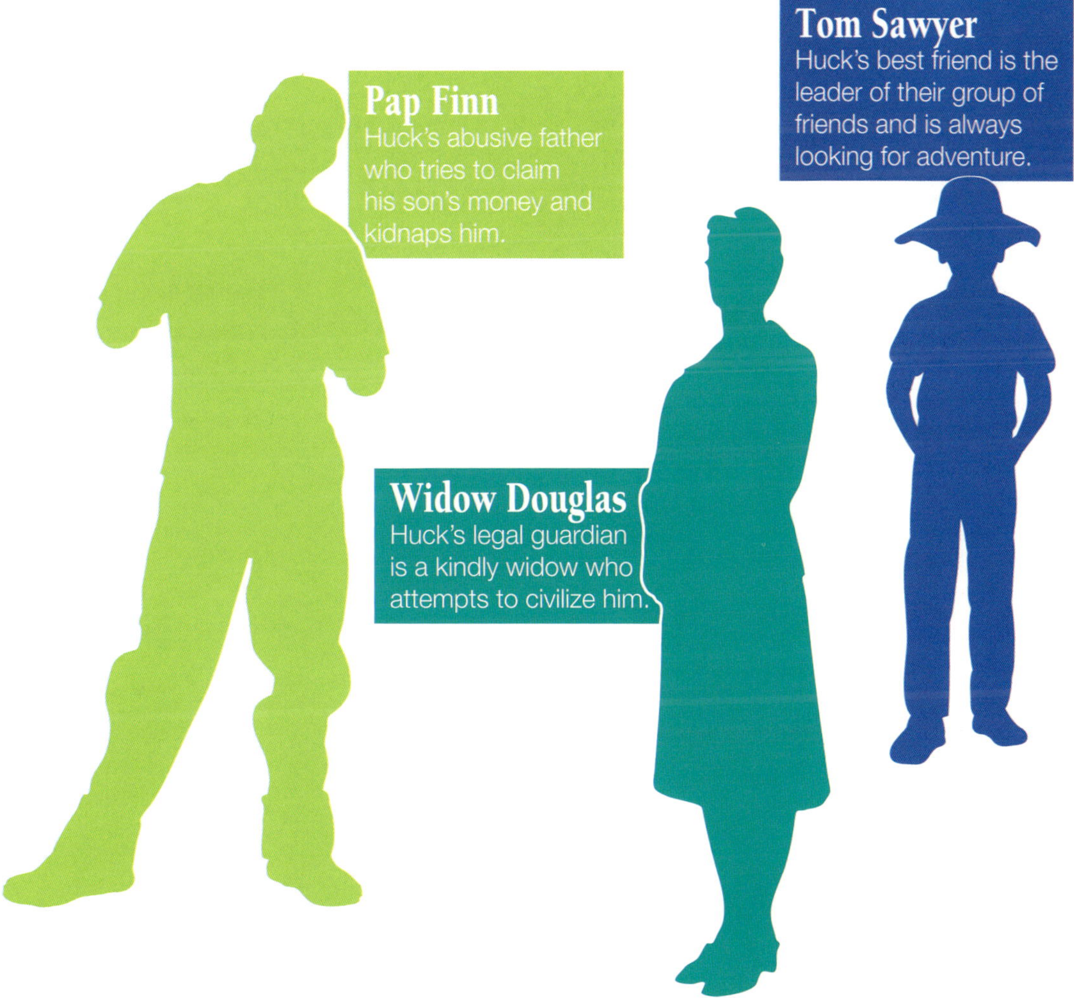

TEACHER NOTES

Document

An Analysis of the Factors Affecting Huck's Growth

Examine this article by Yanxia Sang, published in Vol. 1, No. 5 of the *Journal of Language Teaching and Research* in September 2010.

1. What arguments does the author make? How are these arguments supported?
2. What conclusions does Sang draw in this article? Do you agree or disagree with her? Why? Give reasons for your answer.

More

Character Development in *The Adventures of Huckleberry Finn*

Analyze the characters in *The Adventures of Huckleberry Finn* using the descriptions on the character map and excerpts from each character. Then, choose a character and answer the following questions.

1. Which of the writer's techniques are most effective at revealing this character's traits? Why?
2. In what ways is the characterization of this character ineffective? What could be done to improve this character's function in the novel? Defend your ideas with evidence.

EXTENSION ACTIVITY

Creating a Literary Device Analysis Booklet

Students will analyze the author's use of a literary device in the novel, and create a booklet to present this analysis. An exemplary literary device analysis booklet will meet the following criteria.

- Defines the chosen literary device accurately and in detail
- Places the definition of the literary device at the beginning of the booklet
- Provides strong, specific examples of how this literary device is used in the novel
- Describes examples in detail, with quotations properly integrated
- Includes thorough analysis of the use, purpose, and effectiveness of each example of how the chosen literary device is used in the novel
- Arranges all pages logically
- Examples are organized chronologically
- Provides no more than one example and its analysis per page
- Creates a neat, well-organized, and attractive booklet
- Booklet is colorful and displays the student's creativity
- Uses illustrations to represent the chosen literary device and the examples of how it is used in the novel

The Art of Storytelling

Storytelling is about more than simply recounting a series of events. Great storytellers use literary tools to engage their audience and draw them into the story. Twain is well known for using humor and satire to tell his stories. *The Adventures of Huckleberry Finn* focuses on the serious issue of racism, but approaches it from a lighthearted point of view. Rather than openly stating his views against slavery and racism, Twain creates a series of events that help the audience judge the issues for themselves.

Structure of a Narrative

A story is made up of a beginning, a middle, and an ending. This is known as narrative structure. The beginning of a story introduces the audience to the characters, setting, and basic themes in the story. The middle of a story is where the plot unfolds. Characters encounter situations that drive the story toward a climax or rising action. From its climax, a story begins to wind down toward a resolution. This part of the story is known as the falling action.

Freytag's Pyramid

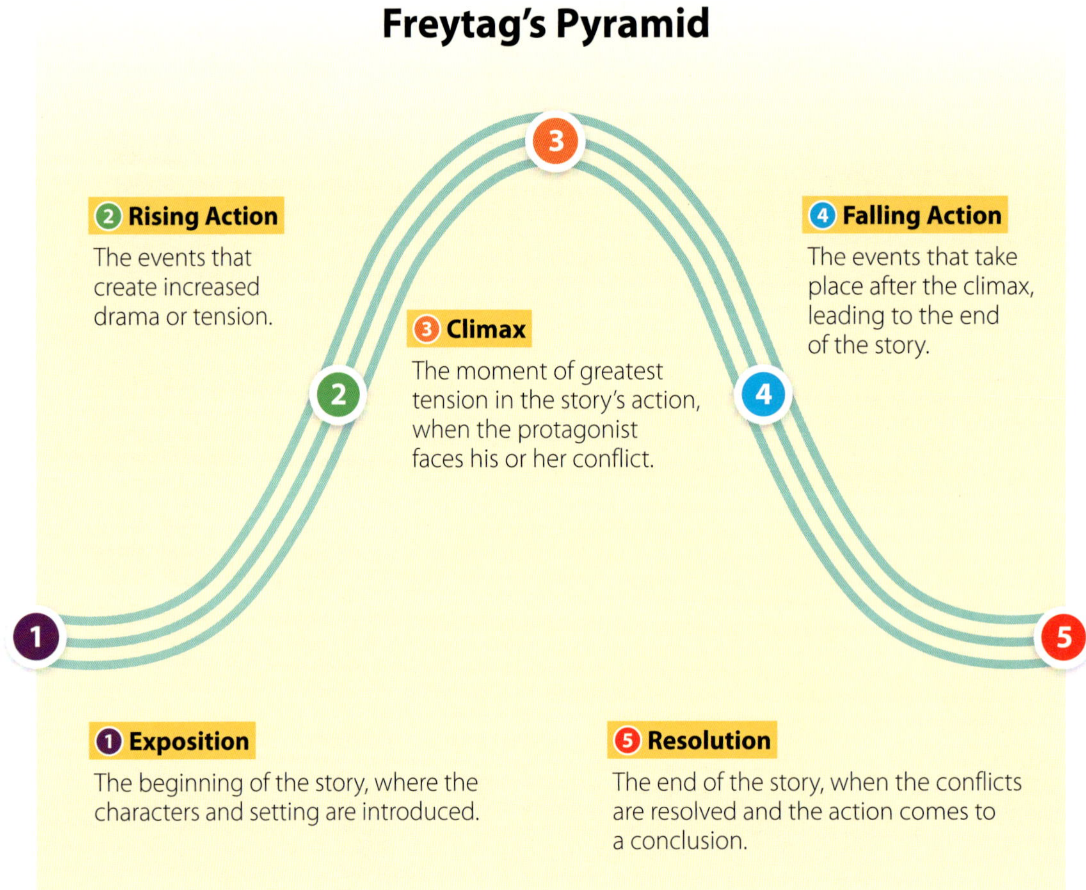

TEACHER NOTES

Plot

Without a plot, a story would be a sequence of random, unrelated events. The plot of a story is what ties the events together. It keeps the story on track, building towards a climax, and ultimately, a resolution. *The Adventures of Huckleberry Finn* follows a linear plot, which presents the sequence of events in **chronological** order. Each event is a plot point creating a sort of timeline of events in the book.

Plot Points in Chapter VII of *The Adventures of Huckleberry Finn*

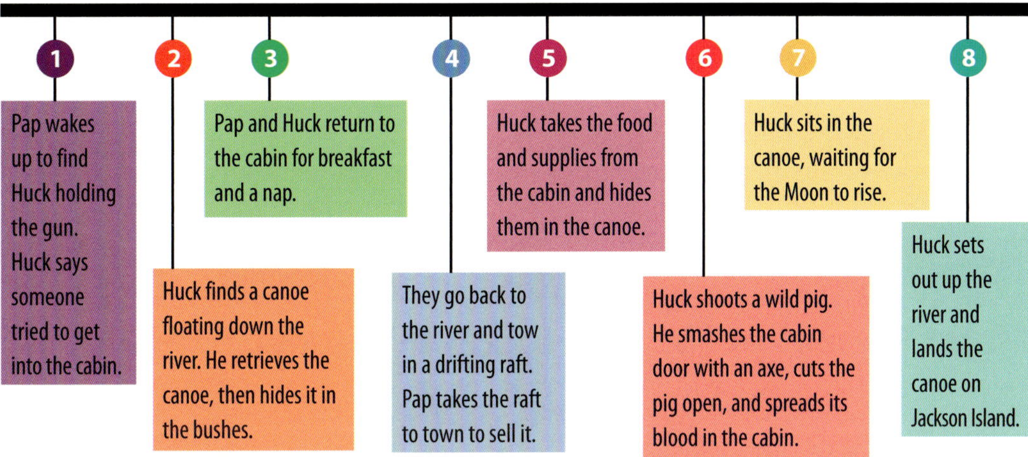

Literary Devices

Writers use tools to create meaning in their writing. These tools are called literary devices. They help readers interpret the work. Literary elements and literary techniques are the two categories of literary devices. Each category is made up of many different tools.

Weblink

An Online Resource Guide to Freytag's Pyramid

Learn how to use Freytag's Pyramid by reviewing this online resource.

1. Explain Aristotle's dramatic plot structure in your own words. How is Freytag's Pyramid a modification of this triangle? In what ways is Freytag's Pyramid a more effective tool?
2. How does *The Adventures of Huckleberry Finn* follow this dramatic structure? Identify where each of the five steps take place in the novel.

More

Examples of Literary Techniques from the Novel

Analyze the author's use of literary techniques and how they contribute to the narrative of *The Adventures of Huckleberry Finn.*

1. Choose one literary technique used in the novel. In what particular way did the author use this literary technique? How effective was its usage?
2. What arguments can be made for the use of your chosen literary technique in a text? If this technique were overused or underutilized, what effect might it have on an author's work?

Theme in the Novel

A theme is a topic, idea, or message discussed in a novel. Sometimes, writers will state the theme at the beginning of the book. Other times, they will wait until the end to reveal the message. Great writers such as Twain develop their themes throughout the story. Plot points advance, characters grow, and themes evolve. Stories with an interesting plot and engaging characters help readers interpret themes.

Values

Characters interpret the plot and theme of a book through their own unique points of view. These perspectives are a reflection of the characters' values. Each character's individual values dictate his or her reactions. In *The Adventures of Huckleberry Finn,* one example where these differing values are illustrated occurs when Huck and Jim come across a steamboat wrecked in the river.

Major Themes of *The Adventures of Huckleberry Finn*

Freedom is a major theme in *The Adventures of Huckleberry Finn*. When Huck spots the steamboat stranded in the river, he wants to board it. Jim would rather sail right past the boat. Both characters long to be free, but they have different ideas of freedom. Huck wants adventure and freedom from the rules of society, while Jim seeks a much more serious kind of freedom for himself, his family, and his people. As each event unfolds, Huck's values evolve.

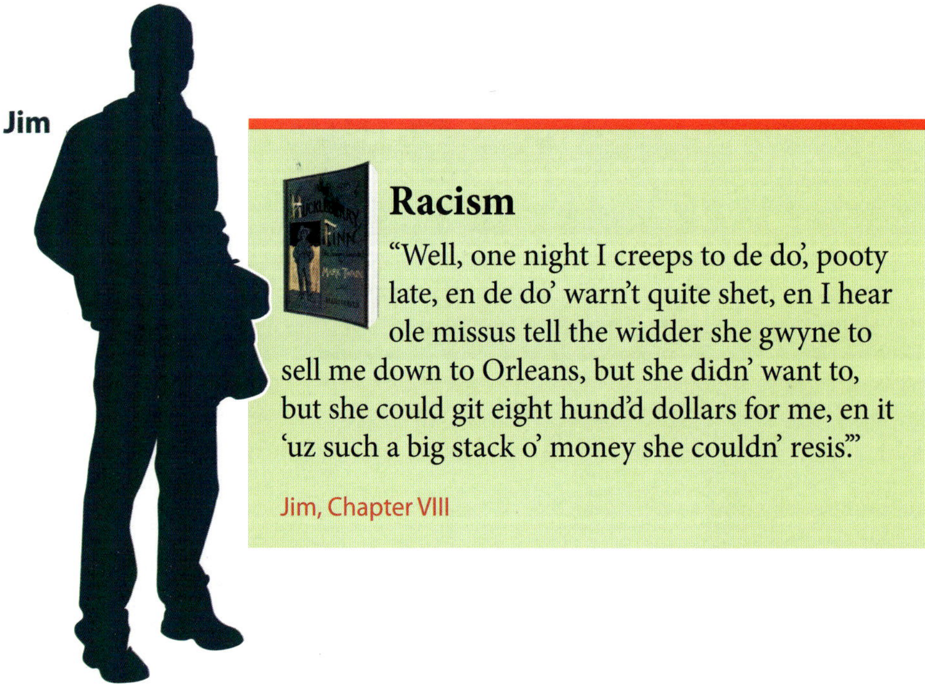

Racism

"Well, one night I creeps to de do', pooty late, en de do' warn't quite shet, en I hear ole missus tell the widder she gwyne to sell me down to Orleans, but she didn' want to, but she could git eight hund'd dollars for me, en it 'uz such a big stack o' money she couldn' resis.'"

Jim, Chapter VIII

Huckleberry Finn

Morality

"I'd see him standing my watch on top of his'n, stead of calling me, so I could go on sleeping; and see him how glad he was when I come back out of the fog; and when I come to him again in the swamp, up there where the feud was, and suchlike times; and would always call me honey, and pet me, and do everything he could think of for me, and how good he always was; and at last I struck the time I saved him by telling the men we had small-pox aboard, and he was so grateful, and said I was the best friend old Jim ever had in the world, and the only one he's got now; and then I happened to look around and see that paper.

It was a close place. I took it up, and held it in my hand. I was a trembling, because I'd got to decide, forever, betwixt two things, and I knowed it. I studied a minute, sort of holding my breath, and then says to myself:

'All right, then I'll go to hell'—and tore it up."

Huckleberry Finn, Chapter XXXI

Jim

Friendship

"Pooty soon I'll be a-shout'n for joy, en I'll say, it's all on account's o' Huck; I's a free man, en I couldn't ever ben free ef it hadn' ben for Huck; Huck done it. Jim won't ever forgit you, Huck; you's de bes' fren' Jim's ever had; en you's de only fren' ole Jim's got now."

Jim, Chapter XVI

Secondary Themes

While major themes may be obvious to readers, smaller themes may be less evident at first. A secondary theme helps to push the story forward. Secondary themes in *The Adventures of Huckleberry Finn* include religion, tradition, youth, and nature.

TEACHER NOTES

Weblink

***The Adventures of Huckleberry Finn* Themes**

Learn more about the themes of the novel by examining this website.

1. Describe how lying is a theme in the novel. Give examples from the text as evidence.
2. How are the themes of loyalty and friendship connected? Which character best exemplifies these themes? Why do you think so?

More

Major and Secondary Themes

Analyze the author's development of themes over the course of the novel.

1. Choose a secondary theme from this spread and analyze its appearances in the novel. How does this theme first emerge? Which is the most poignant example of this theme in the novel?
2. What particular commentary might the author be making about life as a result of this theme's presence in the text? Explain and defend your ideas.
3. Choose a major theme presented on pages 16–17. In what ways does your chosen secondary theme relate to this major theme? Does it deepen or detract from the major theme? How or in what way?

Symbolism in the Novel

Writers will often use symbols to help readers interpret a story. Symbols can include characters, scenery, weather, words, sights, sounds, or any other element of a story. Great authors use symbolism to share their message artistically. Rather than stating an idea outright, an author will use symbolism,which allows the readers to interpret the message for themselves.

Twain's use of symbolism helps him create deeper meanings in his stories. He uses symbols to dramatize, satirize, and humanize his stories. Some symbols in *The Adventures of Huckleberry Finn* are easy to identify, while others require deeper observation. From Huck and Jim to the King and the Duke, each of Twain's characters symbolize a larger part of society or human nature. Natural elements such as the Mississippi River, the islands, fog, lightning, and rain symbolize feelings, beliefs, convictions, and much more.

The Mississippi River

"Well, the night got gray, and ruther thick, which is the next meanest thing to fog. You can't tell the shape of the river, and you can't see no distance. It got to be very late and still, and then along comes a steamboat up the river. We lit the lantern, and judged she would see it. Upstream boats didn't generly come close to us; they go out and follow the bars and hunt for easy water under the reefs; but nights like this they bull right up the channel against the whole river. We could hear her pounding along, but we didn't see her good till she was close. She aimed right for us."

Huckleberry Finn, Chapter XVI

The Mississippi River as a Symbol

In *The Adventures of Huckleberry Finn*, the Mississippi River is a symbol for life and freedom. Huck and Jim take to the river to escape their problems. While the river offers the two characters a sense of freedom, they do not have much control. They cannot control their speed or their route. The raft floats along the path of the river at the speed of the river. This is symbolic of life. As Huck and Jim seek freedom and control over their own lives, they cannot control the passage of time or the natural elements of the world.

EXTENSION ACTIVITY

Creating a Symbolism Poster

Students will choose one of the other symbols listed on page 19 and analyze its role in the novel. They will then create a poster to present their analysis. An exemplary symbolism poster will meet the following criteria.

- Presents a clear purpose that is conveyed throughout the poster
- Shows an understanding of the concept of symbolism and the role it plays in the novel
- Provides an in-depth analysis of what the symbol represents
- Discusses the role the symbol plays in the novel
- Clearly indicates where the symbol appears in the novel
- Uses specific, detailed examples from the text to support the analysis
- Makes clear connections to the text
- Properly integrates all quotations
- Organizes the information in a logical, easy-to-read manner
- Includes high-quality graphics that relate to the symbol and effectively enhance understanding of the topic
- Features clear and concise writing
- Uses correct spelling, grammar, and punctuation
- Clearly labels items of importance
- Headings and subheadings are clear and easy to read
- Uses layout to creatively enhances the information
- Creates a poster that is attractive in terms of layout, design, and organization
- Shows a strong effort by the student

Who Is the Mississippi River?

Other Symbols in the Novel

The Raft

The raft symbolizes escape. It is the vessel Huck and Jim use to escape from the reality of their situations.

The Grangerford House

The Grangerford House is a symbol for the trappings of high society. It is stately, grand, and expensive, but is also old-fashioned and out of place in its less civilized surroundings.

The Snakeskin

The snakeskin symbolizes the traditional beliefs and practices of the people around Huck and Jim. Slavery can be considered one such tradition.

TEACHER NOTES

More

Who Is the Mississippi River?
Assess the author's use of symbolism in the novel.

1. Choose a character from the chart and analyze what the symbol of the Mississippi River represents to him. For which character is this symbol the most poignant in the novel? For which character is the symbol least poignant? Argue your opinions with clear reasons.
2. How is this symbol used or reflected in the novel's themes? Illustrate the ways in which the author's use of language deepens or weakens the meaning of the Mississippi River as a symbol. Explain and defend your ideas.

Weblink

Symbolism
Examine the article to learn more about symbolism in literature.

1. Why do authors use symbolism? How can it enrich a literary work, and the reader's understanding and enjoyment of it?
2. What role has symbolism played in the history of literature?

EXTENSION ACTIVITY

Analyzing a Video

Students will watch and assess a video related to a component of the novel, and write an analysis of the video. An exemplary video analysis will meet the following criteria.

- Identifies the purpose of the video
- Identifies the intended audience of the video
- Describes how the content of the video is presented
- Summarizes the information and opinions presented in the video
- Analyzes the quality of the content presented in the video
- Assesses the effectiveness of the video
- Discusses the technical aspects of the video and whether or not these enhance the content
- Determines whether the images and graphics used in the video relate to the content
- Determines whether the video is easy to follow and understand
- Gives the analysis a clear and consistent purpose
- Organizes the analysis in a logical, effective manner
- Presents a strong, clear argument about the video
- Provides strong and accurate details to support the argument about the video
- Considers other perspectives on the purpose and effectiveness of the video
- Makes connections between the video and the novel
- Properly integrates quotations from the video
- Cites all sources used in the analysis

The Use of Language

Along with his mastery of symbolism, humor, and characterization, Twain was also a master of language. He used language to create a sense of realism. His characters speak the way real people spoke at the time. Twain used slang, accents, and realistic expressions to create relatable characters and believable scenes. *The Adventures of Huckleberry Finn* was groundbreaking at the time it was published, thanks to Twain's use of **dialect**. More than 130 years later, language is still a major focus for the book's critics. Much of the focus, however, is centered around one controversial word found throughout the book. While the N-word is now considered derogatory and offensive, it was used widely in the South during Twain's life. Over time, the language used to describe people of African descent has changed.

Words and phrases used in *The Adventures of Huckleberry Finn*

The author's rampant use of the N-word throughout *The Adventures of Huckleberry Finn* shows how common racism was at the time the novel was written. Rather than using the term as a way of offending, Twain's regular use of the word helps to satirize and ridicule the society he was representing. Many other words in the book were, or still are, considered vulgar, crude, or uncivilized.

Mark Twain's Use of Dialect

"In this book a number of dialects are used, to wit: the Missouri negro dialect; the extremest form of the backwoods South-Western dialect; the ordinary 'Pike County' dialect; and the modified varieties of this last. The shadings have not been done in a haphazard fashion, or by guess-work; but pains-takingly, and with the trustworthy guidance and support of personal familiarity with these several forms of speech.

I make this explanation for the reason that without it many readers would suppose that all these characters were trying to talk alike and not succeeding."

Mark Twain
The Adventures of Huckleberry Finn
Explanatory, 1884

Dialect

Twain's adventurous life and travels brought him into contact with many diverse and interesting people. He had a great appreciation for the differences in each person he met and in each culture he encountered. While he traveled far and wide, it was his adventures close to home that left the greatest impression on the author. Through years of observation, Twain grew to understand the many cultures around the Mississippi River like no writer before. This is apparent through his use of various regional dialects in *The Adventures of Huckleberry Finn*. Twain illustrated these different dialects by deliberately shortening, altering, or misspelling words.

Jim:
"Dah you goes, de ole true Huck; de on'y white genlman dat ever kep' his promise to ole Jim."

Huck:
"I tried to make out to myself that I warn't to blame, because I didn't run Jim off from his rightful owner; but it warn't no use..."

ain't
warn't
govment
sentimentering
by jings
afeard

TEACHER NOTES

Video

The Raft, the River, and The Weird Ending of *Huckleberry Finn*: Crash Course Literature 303

Learn more about the metaphors Twain uses and the ending of the novel by watching this video.

1. Compare and contrast the Mississippi River's beauty with its danger. How does the river set Huck and Jim free, yet also threaten their freedom? Explain this contradiction in your own words and provide examples from the text.
2. What is your interpretation of the novel's ending? Do you think it is a "betrayal of what has come before," as John suggests? Why do you think Twain chose to end the novel in this way?

Weblink

Ishmael Reed on the Language of Huck Finn

Examine the blog post about the language of the novel.

1. Who is the intended audience for this blog post? Is the tone and language used appropriate for this audience? Why or why not?
2. What are the writer's goals and how does he attempt to accomplish them? How successful is he? Why do you think so?
3. Reed claims that, "Mark Twain caught his time and place in a manner that statistics and policy papers can never approach." What does he mean by this statement? Do you agreed with this assertion? Give reasons for your answer.

EXTENSION ACTIVITY

Writing a Book Review

Students will write a book review of the novel. An exemplary book review will meet the following criteria.

- Grabs the reader's attention with a creative headline
- Begins with an engaging lead to pull the reader into the article
- Introduces the title of the novel, the author, and the genre
- Provides a brief plot description that does not give away the entire story, and makes the reader want to learn more about the novel
- Supports arguments about the novel with accurate and detailed information
- Organizes the review and its arguments in a concise, clear, and logical manner
- Fits the format and style of a book review
- Follows the conventions of print or online journalism
- Demonstrates creativity in their approach
- Writes with a unique, engaging voice and perspective
- Provides fresh insight into the novel
- Provides an honest, authentic opinion on the novel
- Gives a clear recommendation on the novel, backed up by specific textual evidence
- Uses correct spelling, grammar, and punctuation

Impact of the Novel at the Time of Publishing

By the time he wrote *The Adventures of Huckleberry Finn*, Twain was already a celebrated author. The novel was considered a sequel to his bestselling book, *The Adventures of Tom Sawyer*. Twain began working on Huck's story in 1876, but was unhappy with his work. He put the story aside for several years and almost gave it up entirely. When he finally published the story in late 1884, the public reception was mixed.

The American Novel

The Adventures of Huckleberry Finn has been called "the first American novel." Many novels were written in the United States before 1884, but *Huckleberry Finn* was the first popular novel to use American vernacular. Most books at the time were still written using literary English. Twain used the normal, everyday language of the people in his book. American writer Ernest Hemingway said, "All modern American literature comes from one book by Mark Twain called *Huckleberry Finn*."

Early Criticism

Critics of *The Adventures of Huckleberry Finn* found many ways to express their dislike for the book. Early reviews of the novel attacked Twain's use of language and morality. It was called "trashy and vicious," "harmful," and "more suited to the slums than to intelligent people." A library in Concord, Massachusetts, became the first to ban the book in 1885.

Positive Reviews

While some reviews were not good, they were not all bad, either. An 1885 review in the *San Francisco Chronicle* called it "the sharpest satire." *The Saturday Review* called Huck Finn a "marvelous" character. Another review described the book as "a string of incidents ingeniously fastened together."

Famous Writer

Twain was considered a celebrity before he wrote *The Adventures of Huckleberry Finn*. His previous stories made him a literary star. His speaking tours and appearances helped sell more books, and finance his business ventures. *The Adventures of Huckleberry Finn*, however, made him a superstar. Twain's friend William Dean Howells said, "Emerson, Longfellow, Lowell, Holmes—I knew them all and all the rest of our sages, poets, seers, critics, humorists; they were like one another and like other literary men; but Clemens was sole, incomparable, the Lincoln of our literature."

Throughout his career, Twain wrote **28 books.**

At least four of Twain's books were published **after he died.**

In 1891, Twain made an investment that lost him an estimated **$200,000.** Today, that amount would equal **more than $5 million.**

TEACHER NOTES

Weblink

Mark Twain's Huckleberry Finn
Explore the website about Mark Twain and his work.

1. Do you agree with the claim that Mark Twain wrote the "great American novel"? Give evidence to support your opinion.
2. Twain has been called "America's Best Humorist." Does he deserve this title? Why or why not?

Document

Saturday Review
[unsigned; Brander Matthews]
1885: January 31
Examine this review of the novel by Brander Matthews from January 31, 1885.

1. What are the main points of the article and how are they presented? Are these points conveyed effectively to the reader? Explain why you think so.
2. What conclusions does Matthews draw in this article? Do you agree or disagree with him? Why? Support your answer.
3. How would you characterize this review? Is it primarily positive or negative? Cite textual evidence to back up your claim.

EXTENSION ACTIVITY

Holding a Classroom Debate

Students will form groups and prepare arguments for a debate on a controversial issue. Exemplary performance in a debate will meet the following criteria.

- Demonstrates in-depth understanding of the topic and related information
- Presents strong, logical, and convincing arguments
- Communicates in a clear and confident manner
- Maintains eye contact
- Uses clear vocal tone and a reasonable rate of vocal delivery
- Uses respectful and appropriate language and body language
- Delivers arguments, evidence, and counter-evidence in an engaging and persuasive manner
- Supports each major point of an argument with several relevant and detailed facts and examples
- Connects all arguments to the overall topic in a clear, concise, and organized manner
- Presents the arguments and supporting evidence in a clear, logical manner
- Presents clear, thorough, and accurate information throughout the debate
- Addresses all of the opposing team's arguments with counter-arguments
- Identifies any weakness in the opposing team's arguments
- Constructs strong and relevant counter-arguments using accurate information
- Presents strong and persuasive arguments throughout the debate
- Summarizes the arguments in the closing statement

Impact of the Novel Now

Although the United States and the world have changed a great deal since Twain wrote *The Adventures of Huckleberry Finn*, some things never change. The novel is considered a masterpiece by many, but still incites controversy in homes, libraries, and schools around the world. *The Adventures of Huckleberry Finn* has been translated into more than 50 languages, and adapted for the stage and screen. More than 200,000 copies of the book are still sold every year and it has become mandatory reading in schools all over the world.

Twain's last **direct descendant**, his ***granddaughter***, **died in 1966**.

In **1976**, an asteroid was named **2362 Mark Twain**, after the author.

Twain was born shortly after the orbit of **Halley's Comet** ***in 1835****. He died during the comet's* ***next orbit of Earth in 1910****. A stamp commemorating the relationship was created by the* ***U.S. Postal Service*** *in* ***1985****, the next time the* ***comet returned****.*

Film Adaptation

The Adventures of Huckleberry Finn first appeared onscreen as a silent film in 1920. Since then, the story has been adapted into many different film versions. In 1993, Disney produced a version called *The Adventures of Huck Finn*, starring Elijah Wood. Intended for a young audience, the film emphasized the adventurous side of the story, but still touched on the bigger moral issues of the book. Disney's version of the story was viewed as a "sprightly, good-humored introduction" to Twain's classic story.

On the Stage

The story of Huck and Jim's adventures on the Mississippi River may seem too big for a stage. In 1985, songwriter Roger Miller proved otherwise. Miller wrote the music and lyrics for *Big River*, a musical adaptation of Twain's novel. The play told the story through original songs, becoming a hit on Broadway. It won seven Tony Awards, including Best Score and Best Musical.

Banned and Edited

Race has always been a major point of controversy surrounding *The Adventures of Huckleberry Finn*. When it was first published, some people thought Twain's anti-slavery attitude was too progressive. Today, some people find the author's portrayal of Jim, and use of the N-word, racist. As recently as 2015, *The Adventures of Huckleberry Finn* has been banned in some American high schools. In 2010, an edition of the book was published in which the N-word is replaced with the word "slave."

Award for Humor

In 1998, the Kennedy Center created the Mark Twain Prize for American Humor. The Kennedy Center is a government organization dedicated to preserving and developing American culture through the performing arts. The Mark Twain Prize honors Americans who have made a cultural impact through humor. The first winner was Richard Pryor. Other winners include Ellen Degeneres, Bill Murray, Will Ferrell, and Tina Fey.

TEACHER NOTES

Video

***The Adventures of Huckleberry Finn* by Shmoop**

Learn more about Twain's use of language in *The Adventures of Huckleberry Finn* and the debate over banning books by watching this video.

1. Do you think Twain's use of the N-word is justified and truthful, or excessive and unnecessary? Give reasons for your answer. Be sure to consider both sides of the debate and try to understand this issue from the opposing viewpoint.
2. Is censorship ever okay? Why do you think so? What would be the effects of eliminating the controversial language from the novel?

Document

***The Adventures of Huckleberry Finn* (1939)**

Read a review by Paul Tatara of the 1939 film adaptation of the novel.

1. Do you think the screenwriter took too much artistic license in adapting the story for the screen? What is the effect of writing Tom Sawyer's character out of the storyline?
2. Why do you think that the film, "fails to capture the real flavor of Mark Twain's time of the Mississippi," as one critic claims?

EXTENSION ACTIVITY

Creating a Timeline

Students will explore a topic related to the novel and create a timeline to present their research on historical events connected to this topic. An exemplary timeline will meet the following criteria.

- Includes the most significant events pertaining to the topic to be compared and analyzed
- Includes interesting events
- Uses accurate information for all events, including date, location, and major details
- Orders the events in a chronological sequence
- Describes each event with accurate, vivid, and specific details
- Presents the topic from three or more perspectives
- Inspires the reader to ask thoughtful questions regarding the events and perspectives presented in the timeline
- Uses correct spelling, grammar, and punctuation
- Presents the timeline in a visually attractive and striking manner
- Presents the timeline in a neat, organized manner that is logical and easy to follow
- Uses creativity to present the timeline in an engaging manner
- Effectively communicates the historical information relating to the topic
- Supports each event with reliable sources
- Expresses a clear purpose for creating the timeline
- Enhances the reader's understanding of the topic
- Includes a correctly formatted bibliography of all sources used to create the timeline

Perspectives on Race Relations

In the years since Twain first wrote *The Adventures of Huckleberry Finn*, race relations in the United States have come a long way. Twain wrote within the context of his younger life, when millions of African Americans were considered the property of others. Much more recently, Americans elected the first African American president. Despite obvious advances, U.S. race relations are still a major source of controversy and tension.

U.S. Race Relations Timeline

1600s

1619 African slaves are brought to the Jamestown Colony in what is now Virginia.

1800s

1847 Escaped and freed slave Frederick Douglass launches an **abolitionist** newspaper, *The North Star*.

1849 Harriet Tubman escapes slavery and becomes a leader of the Underground Railroad.

1861 The Confederacy **secedes** from the Union, partly due to the issue of individual states' rights to legislate on slavery. This starts the American Civil War.

1863 President Abraham Lincoln states that all slaves "shall be free" with the Emancipation Proclamation.

Today, people in the United States of all races, religions, and beliefs enjoy the same freedoms. While this is radically different from Twain's time, America's race issues are far from over. The major issues today involving race relations focus on equality rather than freedom. African Americans, on average, receive less education, earn lower incomes, and are more likely to be **incarcerated** than people of other races. These educational, professional, and judicial differences have lead to tension, anger, and even violence. The United States has come a long way since the days of *Huckleberry Finn*, but it seems there is still a long way to go.

865 The Civil War ends and he Thirteenth Amendment to he U.S. Constitution is ratified, ıbolishing slavery. The Ku Klux ‹lan is also formed.

1868 African Americans are granted citizenship.

870 African Americans are granted he right to vote through the Fifteenth \mendment to the U.S. Constitution.

1900s

1947 Jackie Robinson becomes the first African American to play Major League Baseball.

1954 The Supreme Court rules that **segregation** in schools is unconstitutional.

1955 Rosa Parks refuses to give her seat on a bus to white man. Her arrest leads to the Montgomery Bus Boycott and desegregation in 1956.

1963 Martin Luther King, Jr. leads the March on Washington and delivers his famous "I Have a Dream" speech. The following year, he receives the Nobel Peace Prize.

2000s

2008 Barack Obama is elected as the first African American President of the United States.

2014 Protests and riots break out across the U.S. after an unarmed African American teenager is shot and killed in Ferguson, Missouri.

TEACHER NOTES

Transparency–Timeline

U.S. Race Relations Timeline

Examine the historical and cultural contexts shown on the timeline. Then, contrast and correlate its elements with the themes and events presented in *The Adventures of Huckleberry Finn.*

1. In what ways can historical events, culture, and social mores influence a population's perspective on freedom and equality? How might these elements have shaped the way a reader in the 1880s interpreted the novel?
2. How might the era in which Mark Twain wrote *The Adventures of Huckleberry Finn* have influenced the novel's themes and settings? Where in the novel is this most evident? Explain your reasoning.
3. Which current events, changes in laws, new ideas, or political discussions are shaping freedom and quality in the United States today? Which ideas and attitudes are still prevailing? Why?
4. How might current events and present perspectives affect the way a reader interprets the novel? Why is it important for readers to understand the era and context in which a novel is written?

EXTENSION ACTIVITY

Writing a Comparative Essay

Students will compare two literary devices used in the novel, and then write a comparative essay based on their analysis. An exemplary comparative essay will meet the following criteria.

- Consists of a one-paragraph introduction, three body paragraphs, and a one-paragraph conclusion
- Introduction includes an engaging lead statement about the topic of the essay, more detailed information about the novel, and a one-sentence thesis that specifically states the essay's argument
- Body paragraphs include a topic sentence that refers to the thesis and how the idea appears in the novel, a supporting sentence that points to this part of the novel, textual evidence of this idea from the novel, and analysis of this evidence
- Body paragraphs end with a transition to the next paragraph
- Conclusion refers to the topic of the essay and the three points presented in the body paragraphs, and restates the thesis
- Provides a thorough analysis of the literary devices in question
- Cites strong and thorough textual evidence to support analysis of what the novel says explicitly
- Presents a clear, specific thesis that indicates a high level of critical engagement
- Organizes ideas in a logical manner
- Communicates arguments in a clear, effective manner
- Properly integrates all quotations
- Correctly cites all sources used
- Correctly formats bibliography

Writing a Comparative Essay

The Adventures of Huckleberry Finn features some of American literature's most memorable characters. Choose two characters from the book and make a list of their attributes. Compare and contrast the attributes of the two characters and decide how they are similar or different. Now, write an essay arguing your conclusion. Support your argument with logical reasoning and evidence from the novel.

How to Analyze and Compare Characters

Use the chart to guide your comparison of two characters in *The Adventures of Huckleberry Finn*

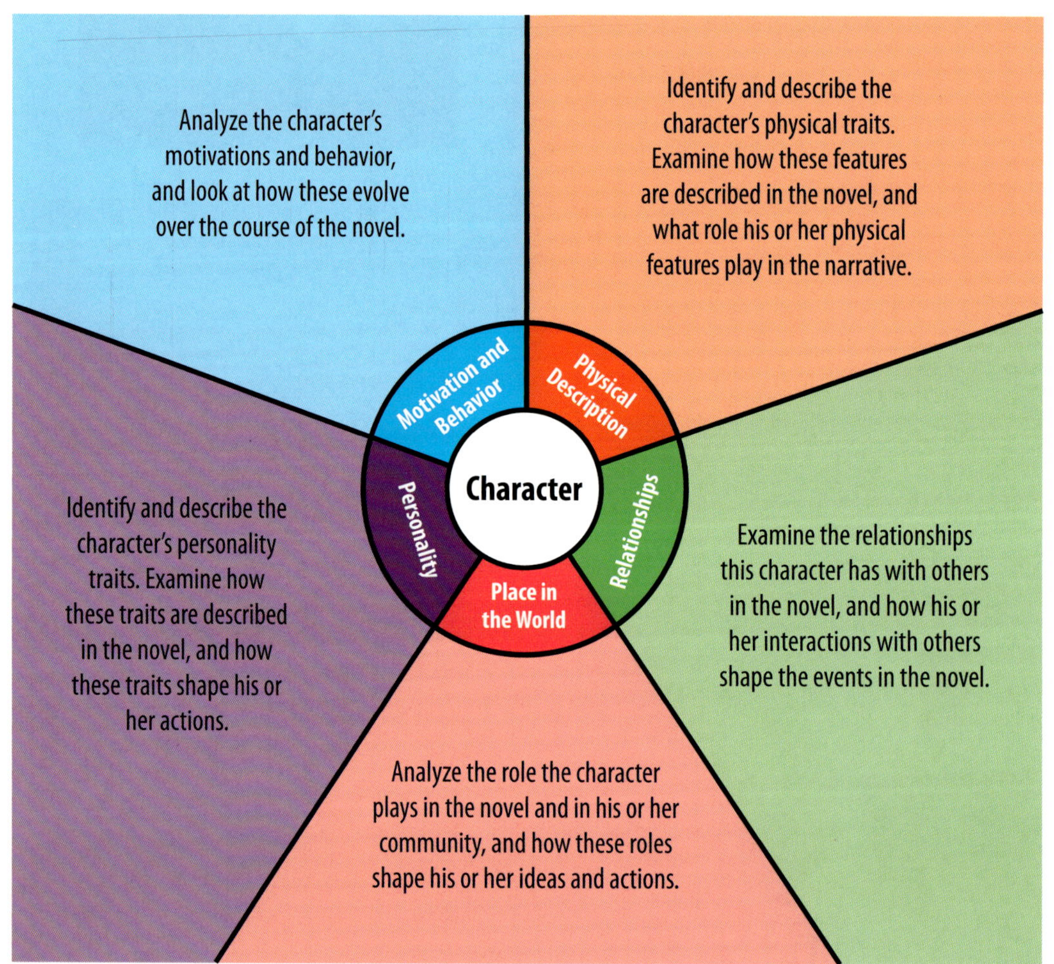

Comparing Huck Finn and Jim

Huck Finn

Personality
- Adventurous
- Mischievous
- Philosophical

Motivation and Behavior
- Protagonist
- Seeks freedom
- Helpful

Place in the World
- Orphaned
- Adopted
- Runaway
- Uneducated

Relationships
- Abused by his father
- Tom Sawyer's best friend
- Jim's companion
- Member of the Gang of Robbers

Physical Description
- 14 years old
- Small and slight
- Barefoot
- Tattered, dirty clothing
- Caucasian

Jim

Place in the World
- Slave
- Runaway
- Well-known storyteller

Physical Description
- Grown man
- Big
- Strong
- African American

Motivation and Behavior
- Seeks freedom
- Wants to buy freedom for his wife and children
- Nervous

Relationships
- Huck's companion
- Miss Watson's slave
- Married
- Father of two children

Personality
- Friendly
- Boastful
- Appreciative
- Caring

TEACHER NOTES

Transparency–Chart

Questions for Character Analysis
Analyze how specific character features, such as conflicts, motivations, relationships, place in the world, and personality affect the plot of *The Adventures of Huckleberry Finn*. Cite strong and thorough textual evidence to support your analysis of what the novel says explicitly as well as the inferences you may have drawn from the novel's setting, themes, and symbols.

Quiz Answers

1. D
2. C
3. C
4. B
5. C
6. A
7. B
8. C
9. C
10. C

Key Words

abolished: ended

abolitionist: a person who believes a practice should end

apprentice: a person who studies a trade or skill

breadwinner: the main earner of money in a household

chronological: in order of time

dialect: a distinct way of speaking in a certain region or area

emancipated: set free

incarcerated: put in prison

secedes: leaves an organization or union

segregation: separation based on race

textile: clothing and fabric

tumultuous: intense or volatile

Underground Railroad: a secret network of safe houses and escape routes for fugitive slaves

Literary Terms

action: everything that occurs in a narrative

antagonist: the character who stands in opposition to the protagonist; in some cases, the antagonist creates or represents the conflict that the protagonist faces

bibliography: a list of sources used in a written work

climax: the height of drama in a story

conflict: a struggle between two or more opposing forces, creating a tension that must be resolved

dialogue: the spoken conversations that the characters have with each other

dramatize: to make more dramatic

exposition: the beginning of the story, where the characters and setting are introduced

falling action: the events that take place after the climax, leading up to the end of the story

Freytag's Pyramid: a narrative structure consisting of five elements; this includes exposition, rising action, climax, falling action, and resolution

hyperbole: exaggeration used for emphasis

idiom: a commonly used expression with a meaning that differs from its literal meaning

mood: the overall feeling that the narrative is intended to evoke within the reader

narrative: a logically arranged series of events presented for an audience; a story

narrative structure: the way a story is built

narrator: the character or person telling the story, providing background information and opinions on the events, and connecting the gaps between major events and dialogue

plot: the specific action that propels a story forward

protagonist: the central character in a piece of fiction who must deal with a conflict and often undergoes some type of change as a result

pseudonym: a pen name or false name used by an author

resolution: the point of the story when the problem is solved

rising action: events leading to the climax

satire: a way of ridiculing society or elements of society

style: the unique way that writers use language to tell their story; this can include word choice, the use of imagery, and the length and organization of sentences

symbolism: a literary technique using symbols to represent and intensify concepts and ideas

theme: the underlying topic, idea, or position in a work that is often a general, universal statement about life

travelogues: stories of travel

Index

LIGHTBOX

SUPPLEMENTARY RESOURCES

Click on the plus icon ⊕ found in the bottom left corner of each spread to open additional teacher resources.

- Download and print the book's quizzes and activities
- Access curriculum correlations
- Explore additional web applications that enhance the Lightbox experience

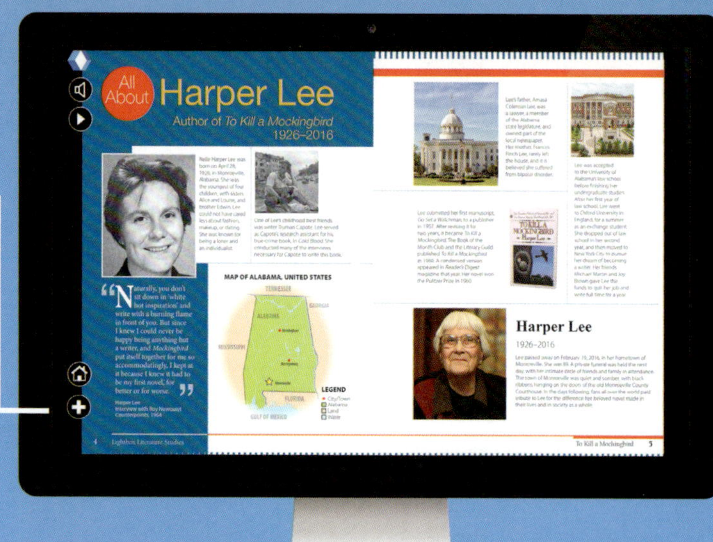

LIGHTBOX DIGITAL TITLES
Packed full of integrated media

VIDEOS

INTERACTIVE MAPS

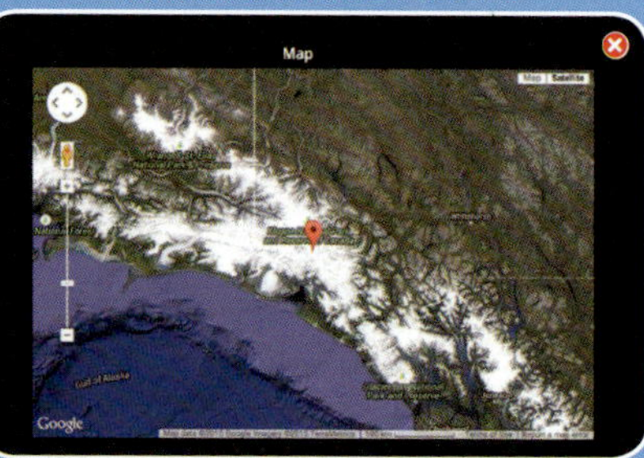

WEBLINKS

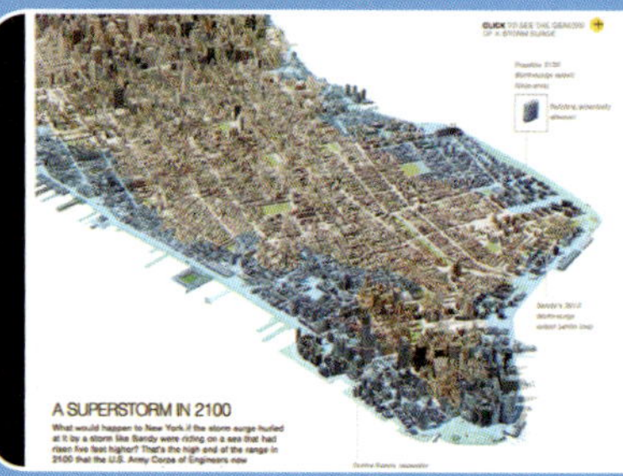

SLIDESHOWS

QUIZZES

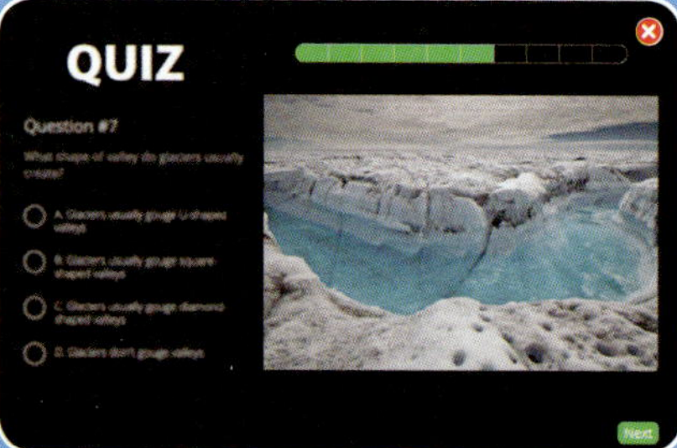

OPTIMIZED FOR

- ✓ TABLETS
- ✓ WHITEBOARDS
- ✓ COMPUTERS
- ✓ AND MUCH MORE!

Published by Smartbook Media Inc.
350 5th Avenue, 59th Floor New York, NY 10118
Website: www.openlightbox.com

Library of Congress Cataloging-in-Publication Data

Names: Wiseman, Blaine author.
Title: The adventures of Huckleberry Finn / Blaine Wiseman.
Description: New York : Smartbook Media Inc., [2018]
Series: Lightbox literature studies | Includes index.
Identifiers: LCCN 2016051613 (print) | LCCN 2017006304 (ebook) | ISBN 9781510520097 (hard cover : alk. paper) | ISBN 9781510520103 (multi-user ebk.)
Subjects: LCSH: Twain, Mark, 1835-1910. Adventures of Huckleberry Finn--Examinations--Study guides. | Boys in literature--Examinations--Study guides. | Finn, Huckleberry (Fictitious character)
Classification: LCC PS1305 .W595 2018 (print) | LCC PS1305 (ebook) | DDC 813/.4--dc23
LC record available at https://lccn.loc.gov/2016051613

Printed in Brainerd, Minnesota, United States
1 2 3 4 5 6 7 8 9 0 21 20 19 18 17

062017
042017

Editor: Katie Gillespie
Art Director: Terry Paulhus

Every reasonable effort has been made to trace ownership and to obtain permission to reprint copyright material. The publisher would be pleased to have any errors or omissions brought to its attention so that they may be corrected in subsequent printings.

The publisher acknowledges Getty Images, Alamy, Newscom, and Shutterstock as its primary image suppliers for this title.